The Sight-reading Sourcebook

Alan Bullard

for

PIANO GRADE THREE

Chester Music
8/9 Frith Street London W1D 3JB

Exclusive distributors:
Music Sales Limited
Newmarket Road, Bury St Edmunds, Suffolk IP33 3YB
This book © Copyright 2002 Chester Music
ISBN 0-7119-9028-x
CH63030
Cover design by Chloë Alexander
Typesetting by Andrew Shiels
Printed in the United Kingdom by
Printwise (Haverhill) Limited, Suffolk.

Chester Music
(A division of Music Sales Limited)
8/9 Frith Street
London W1D 3JB.

PREFACE

This book is for pianists of all ages who wish to develop their sight-reading skills, and contains a number of graded exercises which lead up to examples of tests of similar standard to those set by the major examination boards for Grade 3. The precise requirements, and the way in which the sight-reading tests are offered, does vary from board to board so be sure to check their syllabuses and the specimen sight-reading tests that they publish.

However, good sight-reading is not just about getting good marks in examinations: the skill of sight-reading helps you learn all music more quickly and more accurately. It can save you a lot of time!

Sight-reading and learning a new piece – the difference

Learning to sight-read better will help you learn music more quickly, but the approach to sight-reading is not the same as the approach to learning a new piece. When you learn a new piece you often work at it a little at a time, phrase by phrase, practising it until it is right. But with sight-reading, the aim is to get it right first time! With sight-reading, you *practise in your head*, before the fingers touch the keys, and when you do start to play, you *keep going* (even if you make mistakes along the way).

Keeping going

This is the most important part of sight-reading, and means that *rhythm* - and the basic pulse that underlies it - is even more important than pitch. The exercises in section 1 are designed to help you with this basic skill – keeping the pulse steady: keeping your internal metronome ticking away in time. The three-stage approach suggested in section 1 can be applied to any piece in this book. If you find 'keeping going' difficult, there are plenty of ways to develop it – choose any melody and tap the pulse with one hand and the rhythm with the other; count out aloud while clapping the rhythm, tap the pulse with your foot while playing or singing, even singing any tune you like *in time* with your feet while you walk along the road!

Knowing the keys, getting the notes right, following the shape and fingering

Most music moves by step or in small leaps. Good sight-readers don't work out every note: they make sure that they start in the right place, are aware of the key signature, and then they follow the shape of the music as they move along.

Make sure that you are fluent in your scales and arpeggios. Most examination boards set sight-reading in the same keys as the required scales and arpeggios – so if you know these well, your hands will know the 'geography' of each key, and it will all become much easier! In this book, fingering, where included, is only a suggestion.

Warm up your brain as well as your fingers

Try *beginning* each practice session with a few minutes of sight-reading: get your musical intelligence working as well as your fingers. Try to imagine what the music will sound like *before* you play it. Don't leave sight-reading to the end!

Try, try and try again

If you find an exercise difficult, move back a page or two (or back to Grade 2) and repeat exercises you have already played. Come back to the difficult exercise with renewed confidence!

Sight-read your way to each new piece

Try the 'right first time' approach whenever you are learning a new piece. See how much detective work you can do in your head – phrase by phrase perhaps – before your fingers touch the keys.

The Sight-reading Sourcebook – your passport to saving time and learning more music.

ALAN BULLARD

The Sight-reading Sourcebook – Grade 3

SECTION 1

When sight-reading, always try to work on **both hands together** from the beginning.
The three-stage approach below can be applied to **all** the pieces in this book.

a) Check the tempo and time-signature, and count the **pulse** out loud, counting two bars before you start.
Tap the **rhythms** of both hands at the same time, while continuing to count.

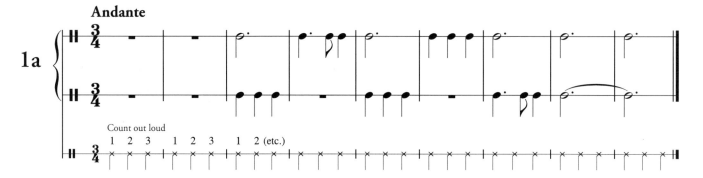

b) Count the pulse quietly and play the rhythms on a single note in each hand, observing the dynamic markings.

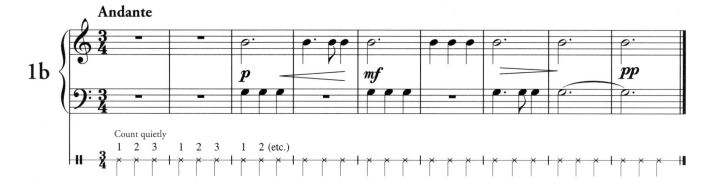

c) Check the **key-signature**, put both **hands in position** over the keys (checking for any changes in position later on), count the **pulse** in your head, and play the complete piece.
Remember to follow the **shape** of the phrases, **don't stop** to work out the name of each note, and let your fingers do the work!

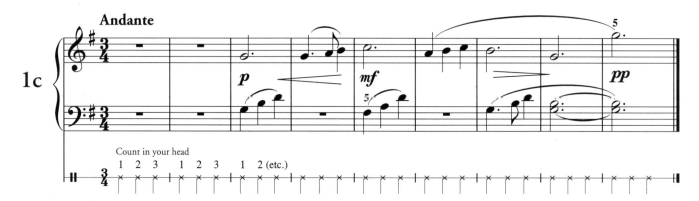

Here's another exercise in the three-stage approach, introducing **compound** time (required by some examination boards for Grade 3) and more **chords.**

a) As before, tap the rhythms of both hands, while continuing to count aloud.

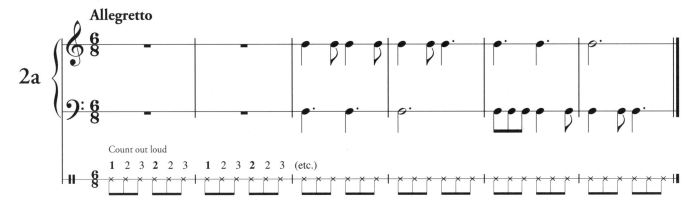

b) Count the pulse quietly and play the rhythms on a **single note** in each hand, observing the dynamic markings.

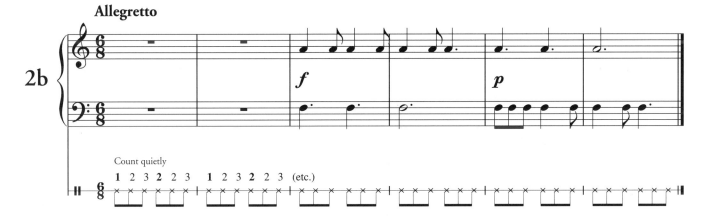

c) Check the **key-signature**, check for changes in **hand position** and unusual fingerings, count the **pulse** in your head, and play the complete piece.

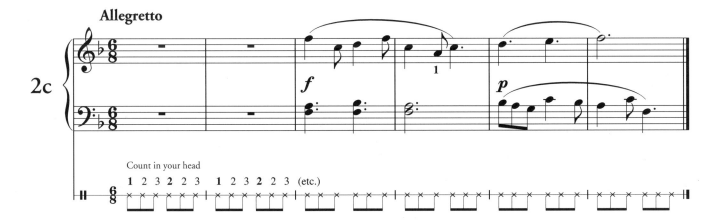

SECTION 2

Thinking in **keys**.
Although these do vary between the different examination boards, this section contains pieces in all the keys that you are likely to need at this grade (apart from C major and A minor) – beginning with G major.

Before each section, make sure that you can play the **scales and broken chords** of the key and don't forget to use the **three-stage approach** to each piece.
Some fingerings are given, but these are suggestions only.

Exploring E minor – make sure that you can play the scale and arpeggio.

Keep hands in position during the rests.

Exploring D major – play the scale and arpeggio first.

Exploring B minor.

Exploring A major.

Exploring E major.

Exploring F major.

Exploring D minor.

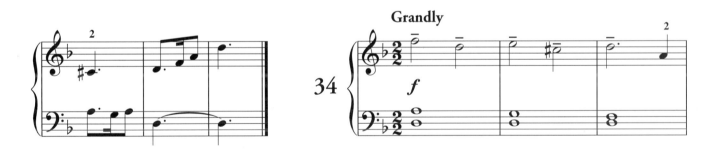

Exploring B♭ major.

Exploring G minor.

Exploring E♭ major – as always, practice the scales and arpeggios first.

Exploring C minor.

SECTION 3

The final section contains slightly longer pieces, including modulations and a range of accidentals.
Remember to use the three-stage approach - particularly b) and c) – as at the beginning of this book.
Some examination boards give you a short time to try the piece out before you play it to the examiner –
use this time to play the rhythm on a single note in each hand and then to try out any awkward
fingerings and changes of hand position. Any fingerings given here are only suggestions.

Rhythmically

54

Slowly and expressively

55

Lively

56

24